# ANOTHER MOMENT
## A Season of Reflection and Identity

By
Jude Ezeilo

Also, by Jude Ezeilo

*Welcome Home: A Memoir*

*The Great Adventures of the Five Little Froggies Volume I*

*Henery Wrenn – The Adventure Begins!*

Published in the United States by Envisionry Media.

Another Moment. A Season of Reflection and Identity. Copyright © 2024 by Jude Ezeilo.

For information contact: _JEzeilo@EnvisionryMedia.com_
_www.envisionrymedia.com_

ISBN 978-1-964776-07-1 (paperback)
ISBN 978-1-964776-08-8 (eBook)
ISBN 978-1-964776-09-5 (hardcover)

To my family, as always. I am grateful and blessed. Always.

To all the immigrants, second sons, and anyone who is struggling with their identity. Your journey may be long and hard. And daunting. Keep strong. Keep going. Keep the Faith. You matter.

To my parents. You are my heroes. My superheroes.

# TABLE OF CONTENTS

My name is Jude.

# CHAPTER 1

Among my other works, I wrote *Welcome Home, A Memoir.* For those who have not yet read it, the book chronicled my path to citizenship, and the struggles and challenges that I encountered along the way. It also outlined my joys and gratitude as I progressed. It displayed the hallmark of a broken immigration system from a different perspective. And some of the good folks who are doing what they can to better it by helping those in need.

*Welcome Home* was a window for my children. Although they were much younger at the time that I was going through the process, which took several years, I wanted a record, an account, a view from my lens of what happened. And I believe that I was able to provide that to them. I know that from experience, when children grow and mature, they develop an interest in the lives and history of their parents and ancestors, those that came before. They, actually many of us, look to the past to help guide us into the future, fill in the gaps, make us complete. In looking back, we get a glimpse of who they were, how they lived, and where we come from. This knowledge has the ability to strengthen, motivate, and propel us forward. It can make us proud and bigger than who we are, or at least who we believe that we are. It also has the ability to stifle, shame or shatter us. It can bring us down, or lay us low. Or in some bizarre and twisted way, it can do some of all of it. It depends on us, who we are, how we choose to see things, how grounded we are – mentally, emotionally, spiritually, and a myriad of other factors. That's the key. More on that later.

The book is also a work of intention and self-healing. I needed to get it all out in order to make sense of everything and understand what it meant, where I fit in, what would come next. And whether it was all worth it. There was plenty of anger, frustration, pain, and sadness. There was also delight, simple pleasures, incredible amazement, and happiness. The enormity of the experience, for me, needed to be detailed and summarized in a way that I could absorb it and draw some perspective. Or at least point me in the right direction. One thing for certain, I found then, as I still truly believe now, that it was worth it, yes.

The process of becoming a citizen did change me. Not just in legal status, but also deeper as well. The road was long and difficult, with so many barriers. Overcoming it gave me a sense of determination and confidence, and I realized that there was not much at all that I could not do if I focused on it. I'm not crazy enough to believe that I got through it on my own. My family was my bedrock and salvation. If not for them, I believe that I would have lost the fight. Again, I thank you all. In the end, I felt whole. Complete. Included. I thought that my full alignment was there and had been achieved. As that chapter in my life closed, I realized after some time that perhaps it was not. I began to understand that to achieve this, it would be a journey, involving more than just change, but evolution. Again, more on that later.

# CHAPTER 2

After the process, as time went on, I became more and more confident with my new citizenship status. I started using "we" more and more, almost like I was originally from here. I was one of "us" now and really embraced it. Why? Because of what I had gone through to get it? Because of all the issues and stereotypes? Because I felt that I deserved it? After all, I'd been here since I was two years old. I'd done all the right things: paid taxes, excelled in school, volunteered, praised the country, stood up for the Pledge of Allegiance, etc. Again, why? Because I felt that I had earned it. I had fought hard for it. I never wavered, although I was knocked down again and again, and the same crap that was used against me was actually tried again. It's all in the first book.

As a new US citizen, I acclimated, emersed, meshed and blended more than I ever had in the past. In my life. I saw things differently (at least I thought I did). I felt things differently (at least I thought I did). I was different than before.

I was a card-carrying member of the club, a true part of the team. I made the cut. I was now an authentic part of the family. Just like my mom, brothers and sisters, and of course my wife. I was a US citizen. Period. I was in and it made a difference. A big difference. And to be completely honest, it still does. Even now, right now.

As I continued, I embraced my newfound status, level and position, and proudly leaned into it. I changed my status at work, also with the Social Security Administration, and I voted. I voted in every election that I could (just once, each time). I received my new passport which I had applied for on the day that I was sworn in as a citizen (you gotta read the first book), and I traveled. I traveled! I went to Jamaica with my amazing wife (lovely time). I went to Guatemala for work multiple times (wonderful people, truly selfless). I went to India, also for work (great people with a very rich culture). I went to Paris with my (again) amazing wife (truly wonderful trip). And I went back to Jamaica with most of the family (it was a blast). Our next planned trip was to go to Europe, but COVID-19 derailed that. Being an American in those foreign lands was exciting and beneficial. I felt that sense of pride and confidence, knowing that they knew where I was from, and I believe that had a hand in how I was treated. It felt good.

I was very much enjoying my new status. I felt both a newness to it, as well as a strong familiarity. It felt good. While I could not run for president (and I think that I would have made a decent one), I could do pretty much anything else, and I acted like it. Or more accurately, I lived it. I wonder if folks who were born here ever feel that. And if they do, is that feeling felt all the time? Constantly? Or just when they see how others don't have what they do. I wonder if those who were born here but live in poverty have that feeling. I guess pride could easily trump poverty (it did for me), but I wonder still. There are those who are definitely in the camp of "America!! Love it or leave it!" They pine for the "good old days"; the way things "used to be"; back when things were "simpler." I tend not to think that things were so good "back then." And those "simpler times" were not so simple for folks just trying to survive. And that the way things "used to be" left a lot of people behind, or simply out and excluded. I tend to favor "America, striving to form a more perfect union." Not that the country is perfect, but that it is like justice, arching in that direction and willing to own her past fully, great achievements and injustices alike. Forever changing, and God willing, evolving.

I felt it. I felt it all. This country's past, her present, her future. The weight, the pressure, the promise. I felt my past, my present, and my future. My struggles, my challenges, my potential. I felt my connection to this place and its connection to me. I felt it in a way that I had not before, and more so than ever. I was a proud American citizen (still am), and I continued.

# CHAPTER 3

Then in April of 2016 something happened. We lost my father to cancer. I lost him. And a part of me shattered and disappeared too. Gone, forever. Prior to his passing, we had learned of his illness far too late. It had spread fast, and fighting it would ultimately do more damage than anything else. As a family, we made a decision. It was the most reasonable, logical, sensible and humane one that we could make. And it was the most gut-wrenching, painful, unfair and difficult one as well. It was done out of love and mercy. And I hope to God that He forgives us for it. The pain is still so very real, even now. Even right now.

My father was many things in his life. I believe that he struggled with the situations and circumstances of his existence. He accomplished many great things, with much to be proud of. And he made many mistakes, some of them very cruel. In the end he was human. Proud, flawed, and all. He was my father. In my book *Welcome Home*, I shared some of our relationship and how we fell out, and ultimately reunited. How he and my mother reunited, and how he was forgiven for that cruelty, and the pain and damage from it. Following that, holidays were more complete with him present. Visits to see my mother would include him being there with her. Special occasions and events would entail my parents showing up and leaving together. As dementia slowly enveloped him, my mother and my oldest sister took care of him and did it all out of love and simple unending kindness.

A couple of days before we lost my father, after we had made the decision that we did, he was moved to hospice care in the hospital. My siblings had flown into town to see him. We all, along with my mother, went to his room. That was the last time that we had all been together, all seven of us. It felt good, and it felt sad.

The next day, my youngest son had a soccer game in the evening at our local YMCA. I came to the field directly from work, and my wife had brought the kids a little later. It was a good game, as I recall, and our son had played well. When it ended, I told my wife that I was going to visit my father at the hospital and that I would be home later. Goodbyes were exchanged with all, and I left. There was something that I had to do. Needed to do, very much. It was essential. I had to go and see my father and share what was on my heart and in my soul. And it had to be done before it was too late. At this stage, he could not communicate, was barely receptive, and was just being kept comfortable. So, I knew that this discussion would be completely one-sided, with me talking and him hopefully listening. I got to the hospital, checked in at the front desk, and went up to his room. As I entered, I saw him lying on the bed, resting peacefully and still. I tapped his leg gently and said hello. He opened his eyes and stared at me for a moment and then settled back to being still, this time looking at me with his eyes half closed. I almost felt bad for what I was about to say, for the things that I wanted to express, and it took more courage than I thought that it ever would. Here he was, dementia had settled in some time ago, and cancer was quickly ravaging his body to the point where he could not speak, and I was still almost fearful to say what needed to be said, because I knew that it would hurt him. But I decided to. I had no choice. I sat down in the chair close to him. And I began. There are some things that I will share here with those who read this book, and some things that are worthy of privacy. This is the latter. As I shared my thoughts and recounted his actions, he moved and stirred. He understood. Fully. I continued sharing my feelings and he continued to react. I know that he was completely with me in those moments, and that it must have been hard to hear, especially from me, who he often called the blessed one. My revealing was not for things that had been done to me, but for someone else. I was clear. And he knew. I then told him the reasons why I had just shared so much. It was because I wanted him to know that I forgave him. For everything. Although I was not the direct recipient of the cruelty of his actions, I needed him to know that I, too, was affected. And that I forgave him. For all of it. I knew that I could not live with not forgiving him until after he passed. That would not be fair to either of us. It would not be right. I wanted him to know before he left us that I held nothing against him. Nothing. In this overwhelmingly unfair situation, this enormously unjust circumstance, at least this one right thing came out of it. Just this one. I feel that upon hearing my forgiveness and expressing my love for this man, that he took some measure of peace with him from that moment forward. At least some. Literally seconds after I had finished speaking, my mother walked into the room. Seconds. She said hello, as she usually does, and upon looking at me, was quiet for a moment. Deep down I sensed that she was somewhat aware of the seriousness of my visit. I said hello back and we chatted for a very short while, as I told her that I was just leaving. We exchanged goodbyes. I took my father's hand and told him goodnight. That was the last time that I saw him alive.

God works in the most mysterious ways. I thank Him for guiding me that day, for giving me the opportunity to have that last conversation with my father. For giving me the courage, for giving him the time, for giving us the moment. Thank You, Lord. I am forever grateful.

The following day, he passed away.

I wrote a tribute to him several years after he passed, on his birthday, and posted it. I'll share that now, here.

*To my Father, on your birthday. May you rest peacefully.*

*You were a:*

*Son*

*Brother*

*Husband*

*Father*

*Soldier*

*Pilot*

*Traveler*

*Student*

*Laborer*

*Graduate*

*Professional*

*Provider*

*Professor*

*Grandfather*

*Minister*

*Retiree*

*And so much more...*

*You were stern - gentle - proud - spirited - stubborn - funny - focused - angry - driven - disciplined - violent - humble - misunderstood - reflective - remorseful - joyous - and so much more...*

*You gave, sacrificed, protected, defended, challenged, overwhelmed, supported, taught, confronted, subdued, repented, evolved, overcame, diminished, shined, loved, and so much more...*

*You lived. You mattered. You passed.*

*I drink a toast to you thru teary eyes, and I will always love and miss you. Always.*

There are far too many memories that I have of him, that I had with him, to share here now, in this writing, that would do any molecule of justice to him, to us, to me. I'll suffice it to say that through it all, he was my father. In all ways, he was my father. Take that as you will.

# CHAPTER 4

Following, something changed in me. Many things changed within me. Something that I was not aware of fully was altered. Something connected to my identity, my sense of self. I thought that it might have, must have been the loss of my father, my ancestor, my lineage. After all, that would seem reasonable under the circumstances. But something else, different, unique shifted within me. I felt off again. But again, I thought that was to be expected, especially given the myriad of emotions that I was experiencing at the same time. I wouldn't understand what it was until much later. And I continued.

There is a hole in my heart where he once was. I missed him so much then, and still do now. I completely believe, and fully realize that he has gone to his reward, to be with his fathers, our fathers, the Father. Even with this knowledge and faith, I miss him. Five years after his passing, I made a decision to celebrate his memory and his soul uniting with the Creator, and the joy that he must be feeling in paradise. But I still feel the loss. I've resigned myself to the reconciliation of the joy and pain of this for me. Even with the eternal bliss that I feel that this man now enjoys, I also feel a sadness that I believe will not ever truly fade from within me. And that's okay. That balance is met.

I visit with him, with some occasional frequency. The cemetery is under 30 minutes away. And when I do, and I share, I feel his presence, his essence. And I am in a way comforted.

There were times that I visited him and was accompanied by my youngest. I cherish some of those moments. Indeed, there were times that I would go without her, and when she found out that I did, she would become angry with me for not taking her. This little soul, since the day of her birth, never ceased to amaze me. Ever. And still continues to, to this very day. After losing him, I knew that I'd never be the same. And I'm not. And that's okay.

My visits these days are by myself, sitting on our family bench, under that large tree, being in just the moment, hopefully achieving some sense of peace.

Just after his passing, and that first meaningful impacting Christmas that followed, one without him for the very first time in my entire life, a new year had begun. And I continued.

# CHAPTER 5

In January of the new year, something wonderful happened. My first book, *Welcome Home, A Memoir* was published. The launch actually caught me by surprise. I was working with the publishers right up until the very last moment. I had made some changes and additions to the work and was not sure that they could or would be incorporated into the final product. I had actually resigned myself to the possibility that I had missed my window. But, as things turned out, I had not. The revisions were incorporated, and the work completed. I was very happy with the results. Still am. The feeling was awesome. Still is. My excitement was matched only by my gratitude. Not just for the folks at ABP, the publishers, who had embraced my story, and with it me as well, but for the ones who made me who I was, who I am, and who I will ultimately be and become. The folks who know me best and love me most. The dedications page in that book are some of the most sincere and heartfelt words that I have ever chosen to share. Again, to you all, I extend my everlasting appreciation and everlasting love.

The year was full of memorable moments. Ups and downs. Some things of note were a trip to Jamacia with most of the family. To travel to this place (for the second time actually for my wife and me) was a joy. It also provided a contrast of sorts. We were staying in an all-inclusive resort, and apart from them taking hours to ready our rooms (such a long wait), it was a great place. The food, the drinks, the activities – night and day, were all top-notch! We truly had an amazing time. We took several excursions that included climbing a waterfall, ziplining through a jungle, bobsledding down a mountain, traveling up to other mountains to different waterfalls and experiencing hot springs, enjoying local cuisine, exploring, and so much more. Truly an amazing time. However, the resort that we stayed at was guarded. Heavily guarded. Unless you had a real reason to be there, you were not allowed to enter – no exceptions. We were also told not to wander about outside certain areas, including the resort. I took that as basic safety. Just being cautious, perhaps overly cautious. But it was more than that. We were told that it was simply not safe. At all. I recall hearing this, and indeed seeing some of the poverty that presented itself on the shuttle ride from the airport to the resort. I also witnessed this on our many excursions, both to and from the resort. These people looked like me, like us. And yet there were very real concerns for our safety. I understood it, to be sure, but it still weighed on me. What was the difference between us and them, except for our nationality? Our origin, as it pertained to where we resided? Perhaps our economic conditions? Apart from that, nothing. We were strangers here, not a part of this land, and its history and culture. While we did partake and enjoy its truly rich customs and heritage, its beautiful lands and wonderful folks (the ones that we encountered), we were not, and likely could not be anything but strangers, visitors, different. That had an impact on me that would not fully be explored deeper, until later.

Also, throughout that year we traveled within the US for milestones and family gatherings, engaged in some major home renovations, and witnessed a solar eclipse, in addition to the usual day-to-day activities that defined and consumed our lives. Normal stuff.

Later that year, we saw and tracked on the news, with the rest of the country, at least the east coast, the formation and strengthening of Hurricane Irma. This storm was a major concern, as it was forecasted to head right up the east coast of Florida as a Cat 4/Cat 5 major storm. We had family discussions, and the decision was made to evacuate the state. And we did. We rented a large van, packed ourselves and extended family up, and headed north to Georgia a few days before the storm was slated to hit. Unfortunately, we were not the only ones with that same idea. Not at all. While the gas stations were systemically running out of gas, as they always did when a big storm approached, the roads were something else entirely. The journey north, which we had made numerous times before, as we had family there and would routinely visit, was extremely slow going. It seemed like thousands and thousands were evacuating the state at the exact same time. The exact same time. The trip took over 21 hours!! My wife did an incredible job getting us there safely. She's a hero! We arrived the next day, checked into a very nice hotel, celebrated a milestone birthday for one of our children that very morning, and then slept (and slept and slept).

The trip actually turned out to be a lot of fun. We even saw other family friends who made the same decision and journey. There were moments of guilt as I wondered how the folks and family still in South Florida were doing. I reached out from time to time, and they were safe. And busy. In Atlanta, where we ended up, we took in the sights, visited places that we'd never been to before, met up with family members on both sides, and enjoyed some high-quality time with them. We also celebrated another milestone birthday for another one of our children there too. We were safe and together. And that made things okay.

When it was time to leave, after the storm had passed, we headed out very early, still overnight. The hope was to beat the traffic heading back down south. Nope. Again, it seemed like everyone had the same idea. We left the hotel and eventually made it to the highway. The trip was smooth at first, but then we hit traffic. A solid wall of it. Almost unmoving. And when it crept forward, it was at a snail's pace. Just plain slow. This time it took us about 20 hours to get home. Again, we were cloaked in the cape of my wife's steady driving. Again, our hero.

The trip highlighted to me just what we can do when faced with something bigger than us. We all pitched in and stepped up. Everyone pulled their weight. I'm always amazed at how coming together for a common cause usually brings out the best in folks. We were no exception. I was proud of us on that occasion, as I had been on countless ones before, and indeed afterwards too. And more was sure to come. And did.

The rest of the year was getting back to our sense of normal, whatever that was, and taking things one day at a time. No real choice with that. There were major changes throughout the year, from start to finish. And we continued.

# CHAPTER 6

Work, school, special events, occasional milestones, usual routines, normal nonsense, etc. Time passed, and things progressed. We were all getting back to and continuing life and living. In October of 2018, at the YMCA, I was playing basketball in a league. The players were much rougher and, to a degree, violent. This was not like the office/work league where I played for ten years before, won 2 championships and 1 second place (all with an excellent group of guys), all professionals (well mostly), and we had to work together the next day. At the YMCA, there was no such thing.

During the game, a game which had grown in physicality and aggression, I jumped and got a rebound. As I went back up for what should have been an easy layup, I was fouled hard by a player (a fool who thought that he had skills, or just a chip on his shoulder for getting beat off the ball more than a few times; who knows) on the opposing team. When I say "fouled hard," I mean that it was a dirty, cheap shot. This player jumped up to block my shot. He had no chance of this, given that I was several inches taller, and already up in the air. So, he did the next worst thing. He did not jump in the direction of the ball, he jumped directly at me, and using both arms fully outstretched, he jumped directly into me, slamming down on my shoulder with his full body weight. I was already up in the air, my arms outstretched, completely exposed. When he struck me, the pain was immediate and intense. It was blinding. My shoulder felt like it had been battered with a baseball bat or a heavy mallet. As I came crashing down, I don't recall if I cried out; there was just so much pain. I could not lift my left arm for what seemed like an eternity. The ref blew his whistle, called a (flagrant) foul, and I got to shoot free throws. I could barely lift my arm. The shots were flat. And meaningless. I knew something was definitely wrong. The pain would not go away. I don't recall if or how I finished the game. I do remember driving home, left shoulder on fire, using only one arm.

After a few days of Tylenol, icing and elevating, it had gotten worse and worse. I saw my doctor, and he referred me to an orthopedic surgeon. After tests and scans, it was confirmed that my left rotator cuff was torn, as well as part of my labral. Surgery was scheduled for mid-January 2019, the 16th.

The surgery went well, and the pain was far less than when I had my other rotator cuff surgery several years earlier. This current procedure was still painful but more bearable. I recall after that previous surgery, when I was recovering my parents stopped by my home to see how I was doing. It was unexpected, thoughtful, and very kind. I felt much better after that. This current time my mother did come by and visited. She brought me some clothes to wear with the brace that I was given after the procedure (my arm and shoulder needed to be completely immobilized) and offered some good advice about the meds. As an RN (and a mom, my mom), her advice was material and taken. I felt better very soon afterwards. This was also very much due to my wife's constant care as well as my second son's attention. He took great care of me that first day when I came home, by keeping me on schedule with my medication as well as always making sure that I was hydrated. Overall, I was in excellent hands, full stop.

Much of the remainder of that year was spent on recovery. First, six weeks (six LONG excruciating, tedious, uncomfortable weeks) of an immobilizing brace – at home, at work, everywhere. Then multiple checkups, which led to two more weeks (two More!!) of wearing the brace "just to be sure." Actually, because of the brace, I slept in a chair (yes, eight weeks of sleeping in a chair almost every night). Over time, because of my position in the chair, and how much pressure I had put on my right elbow, as I was still wearing the brace on my left shoulder and arm, it caused some nerve damage because of the restricting flow of blood to my right hand. This led to me seeing another specialist. He ran tests (which were painful, and a little bloody) and confirmed that there was definitely nerve damage, but that it should heal over a very long time (I still feel it, so it's still healing, but very much better). More surgery was offered to correct it quicker, and was declined (no, thank you very much).

Afterward came several months of physical therapy, several times a week. Everyone who "worked" on me was professional and polite. They did their jobs well. My two main therapists were fantastic. Their techniques were very good, but their attitudes and personalities were excellent. Both had stories to share and did so extensively every time that I was there. They made me laugh, a lot, sometimes through the pain. Although I showed my gratitude with gift cards and thank you notes during my last session, I'll always be grateful for the welcome and laughter that they showed and shared with me.

While it took a very long time before I was able to really get back into the gym, I credit my success to the doctors, nurses, medical teams, PTs, and of course my family who supported me, and put up with a Lot!

# CHAPTER 7

Following 2019 and the surgery, PT and healing came 2020. And that's when it all changed. Everything.

The year started out very well. We were lucky (and skilled) enough to get tickets to Hamilton, the musical, at the Kravis Center in West Palm Beach. It was fantastic! It very much lived up to the hype, all of it. It was exciting, infectious, moving, funny, smart, etc. Very well worth it. At work, there was a special speaker who came to our corporate campus headquarters, and I was fortunate enough to see and hear her. It was Deborah Roberts, the famous journalist. She shared stories of her experiences, including her education, early up through current career path, life changes, and family, including her also famous husband Al Roker. She was very informative, and more inspirational. The kids were doing well in school, with one getting ready to go off to UCF for college later that year. And my mother had knee surgery, which went well.

Following her surgery, I would go to see her every evening after work, first in the hospital and then eventually in the rehab center. We would talk, and eventually watch the news which began reporting on this "thing" that was slowly beginning to happen and spread. At first it was on a cruise ship, and then, little by little, and more and more, it began to spread. We talked about it every night as we watched the news. And it seemed to get closer and closer. The Coronavirus. COVID-19. It was here.

At work, we were directed to make preparations to ensure that each of our teams and direct reports could work from home, if we needed to.

At school, precautions were made, and systems were tested to ensure that the kids could learn from home, and that teachers could teach from home, if they needed to.

Overall, there was a lot of anxiety, stress, fear and tension throughout the communities and county. On the evening of March 12th, a Thursday, I was at my youngest son's chorus and band musical concert. It was in the school gym and followed a more-so regular day of learning and prep. He (actually all of them) played great, and I enjoyed it very much. The very next day was the last day of in-person school for the rest of the academic school year. The kids were informed at school. On Saturday the 14th, we received an email from the principal stating in part:

*Good afternoon...Parents/Guardians, and Students.*

*In this time of uncertainty and rapidly evolving events the Palm Beach County School System has elected to close schools this coming week, and the following week, which was already scheduled as Spring Break. We, of course, will follow this same schedule in an abundance of caution to protect the health and well-being of all our students.*

*Please note the Coronavirus Alert on the Homepage of our website. It is filled with information on the latest news, especially as it pertains to school.*

Again, school was closed for the rest of the academic year. The virus was spreading.

Also on the 14th, in the afternoon, I received an email from work stating essentially that the building was closed until further notice, due to the COVID-19 virus. My office shut down. Their school shut down. Most of the world shut down. It was unlike anything I, or anyone else I assume, had ever seen or experienced before.

We eventually took the kids for a drive around. It was like a ghost town, everywhere. The parks, the parking lots, everywhere. Empty or almost baren. Later as my wife or I went shopping, in the stores, supplies were already flying off the shelves. My barbershop closed, as did many other places. School went virtual on March 30th.

We all watched as the case counts just kept getting higher and higher. As did the hospitalizations, and eventually the deaths that followed. On April 3rd, in the US, there were 261K cases and 6,699 deaths in total. That number would climb to over three thousand deaths every single day. Every single day. We were told to wear masks and social distance. We renovated the house to accommodate five people working and schooling from home. And the world waited as the world came together to find a vaccine.

We moved forward, one day at a time. It was strange and a little scary with this virus, but we were together. We acclimated and remained positive. We followed the science. We stayed vigilant. And more. We made the best of it, as we often did.

During that time, there were some very special moments and events that created some very special memories. This was despite the darkness of the virus that was increasingly spreading. Some of those times included my 50th birthday. A true milestone. On that day, I wrote and posted the following:

*50 And Beyond…*

*Today I turn 50 years old. A full half century. A first step into the golden years. A milestone. In some cultures, that would be considered a great accomplishment to be celebrated, a rite of passage, an honor. In others it's considered over the hill, the beginning of the end, or just plain old.*

*I will admit that for some time I had trouble with this. I struggled as the day approached. I even dreaded it, to a degree. Was my youth spent? Could I ever consider myself young again? Was I just plain old? I struggled.*

*But then I realized that unless that day came and went, I would miss out on, or not be a part of, some of the most wonderful and special things and events still yet to come. So, I reflected on it heavily, and prayed on it solemnly. And this is where I landed.*

*Unless I turn 50, and beyond, I will never see my sons, or daughter graduate high school. Or any of my children graduate college. Ever incredible young souls.*

*Unless I turn 50, and beyond, I will never see any of my children marry and be truly happy, as I did, and as I am.*

*Unless I turn 50, and beyond, I will never become a grandfather – okay, I can wait another decade before that happens, no joke.*

*Unless I turn 50, and beyond, we will never make it to 50 years together, my amazing wife and me. And we're already halfway there. I adore you.*

*Unless I turn 50, and beyond, the next book will never be published, and it's almost done.*

*Unless I turn 50, and beyond, I will never see the end of this new norm, given the current environment, and the newer norm that will follow. Stay strong folks, we'll get thru this together.*

*Unless I turn 50, and beyond, I will never see all the friends and family, the acquaintances and loved ones again. Ever. That's reason enough to look forward to this.*

*Unless I turn 50, and beyond, I will not be witness to the beauties and wonders and splendor that God has in store for me, that He has entrusted me to take care of, that He has truly Blessed me with in all ways, every day, and always.*

*So, I turn 50 with this knowledge and wisdom. I turn 50 with joy in my heart. I turn 50 with the grace and miracles bestowed on me from on high. I turn 50 with the true spirit of the day, and beyond.*

And so, I did. And so, I do.

There was also the family time that organically occurred by virtue of us being together in that way. Over that summer, in the afternoons and into the evenings, we would bring out the portable basketball hoop that the kids got for Christmas just a few months earlier (and put together themselves!) and play and play. Each man or woman for themselves. Our oldest, who had since moved out (prior to the pandemic) would often stop by and fully engage. The games got a little testy and competitive from time to time, but they were incredibly fun. And bonding. I had to "school" the young bloods (although I'm sure that they'll say that it was the other way around). Folks from the neighborhood would come out to watch us play, or if they were walking by, they would cheer us on (or offer advice on moves). We usually finished far after the sun set, and we could barely see anything. Tired and worn out, we would end for the night (and sometimes order dinner to be delivered). We were blessed with the time that we had together.

Other special events included a first-time voter voting, a (virtual) high school graduation, starting college (again virtually), and just being together. It was a very good summer for us, despite the other things going on.

# CHAPTER 8

We were of course always tuned into the news, constantly keeping up with the testing, rates (infections, hospitalizations, deaths) and where the scientists were with the potential vaccines. Any and all progress was swiftly turned into marked enthusiasm, and more so hope. I personally felt that things would get better. How could they not? The whole world was going through this at the very same time. Resources from what seemed like everywhere were laser-focused on beating this thing. And by the grace of God, we were okay, right then, right there.

But something else also occurred that had a profound impact on so much, and so many. In late May, around the 26th, a video emerged showing the murder of George Floyd, by a police officer. This did not occur during a gun fight. This did not occur while Mr. Floyd was fighting the police. This did not occur because the police officer was defending himself, or the public at large. No. It occurred because the police officer deliberately and intentionally put his knee on Mr. Floyd's neck, and effectively slowly suffocated him to death. This occurred while Mr. Floyd had his hands cuffed behind his back. This occurred while Mr. Floyd was lying down, face down, on the street. This occurred while Mr. Floyd repeatedly begged for help, air, life, stating over and over again "I can't breathe. I can't breathe." This occurred while crowds gathered, watched and recorded the episode in real time, as the police officer barely moved, and Mr. Floyd slowly died. Or more accurately, was slowly killed.

Bystanders witnessing this screamed and called out everything that they could in order to try and get the police officer to cease. It didn't work. They shouted obscenities at the police officer. It didn't work. They called the police on the police officer. It didn't work.

And perhaps the most haunting, hateful aspect of this murder was the simple straightforward gaze of complete indifference that the police officer wore throughout the whole encounter. As if it meant nothing to him. As if there was no worth to the man beneath his knee. As if Mr. Floyd's life utterly didn't matter. Not one damn bit.

Seeing that markedly shocked me, and it didn't. I was surprised, and I wasn't. I was angry, and I felt it hard. I had a difficult time processing what I was watching. Was I seeing this right? At first, I just watched. The news announcer had already explained what was about to occur. Additionally, I had already heard about what happened. But to see it... To actually witness it... To be taken there as it unfolded... Almost unbelievable.

What the hell was I looking at? Nothing prepared me for what was unfolding on my television, right there, right then. At first, I just watched, not fully knowing what the next moment would be, nor the next, nor the one after that. Then I found myself reaching out from the inside, willing that officer to get off Mr. Floyd's neck. Get off his neck. Get off it, dammit! Now!! Move!! Damn you, move!! You're killing him! You're killing this man!! He's helpless! Move!! Don't you hear everyone?! Get up!! Move!! Goddamn you, MOVE!! Then nothing. Nothing from Mr. Floyd. No words. No movement. No life. Nothing. From him. From me. No words. No movement. No sound. Nothing. Numb. And then it came. Wave after wave, stronger and stronger. Sheer open anger. I felt my heart beating, my chest pounding, my breath ringing loudly in my ears, in my head, in my soul. "Damn it," was all I could muster as my head shook slowly from side to side. "My God, he's dead. He just killed him. What?"

Nothing made sense. That made no sense. Why would he do that? What was the point? The man was already down, on the ground, handcuffed. Begging for his life. Why keep your knee on his neck? I was confused. The man was already down on the ground. Why keep applying pressure? The man was already down, on the ground in handcuffs. What were you doing? Didn't you hear the crowd? People yelling that he'd passed out? To stop?

The man was already down, on the ground in handcuffs, hands behind his back. Why keep going? Everyone was yelling at you to stop. At least check him out.

The man was already down, on the ground in handcuffs, hands behind his back, begging for his life.

Damn it. Damn you. You knew. You knew exactly what you were doing. Exactly what you were doing. No, you weren't trying to intentionally kill him in cold blood right then and there, in front of these people, in front of the world. That takes an insane amount of madness, and that's not you. No. What you did was far worse. The message, the truth, that I took from the look on your face as it happened was that this man, this human, this life, was nothing to you. Nothing at all. Worthless. Chaff, as my father would say. This chained man was unworthy of any compassion, any caring, and beneath any and all contempt. You stood there open and proud, wearing that badge and uniform, mocking law, order and justice. You coward. You knew exactly what you were doing. You weak coward, you knew.

My anger never went away. Never diminished. I saw it reflected and amplified in marches, protests and demonstrations throughout the country and overseas. So many saw. And felt. And as I watched this continue, and supported it, I also knew that this, for all the attention that it was receiving – and rightly so – that this was neither new nor unique. On the contrary, it was far too common. This thing that happened was not rare. This thing was part of the cloth woven into the fabric of our, of this, society. This thing was real, and it was frighteningly far-reaching, and sad and shameful. But it was not new. So many had spoken about this thing for so long. So many had given, no sacrificed, so much for so long. So many had lost far too much for far too long because of this thing. This thing. Define it as you want. As I see it, it is the belief that certain people are simply worth less than others, deserve less than others, matter less than others. This thing, this belief, is the cornerstone, foundation, and bedrock of bigotry, discrimination, and racism. It permeates every facet of our society – education, religion, economics, etc. And now, through this, it was everywhere and could hardly be ignored or dismissed.

Marches, protests, demonstrations, speeches, discussions, meetings. It was everywhere. People were "taking a knee" in droves. Athletes, performers, influencers, organizations, etc. Everywhere. While this thing was old, very old, this response was not. It was new, powerful and motivational. And hopeful. The world seemed to be watching. In the middle of a pandemic, taking thousands of lives every day, everywhere, the world was watching.

Here at home, an opportunity was taken for further understanding of this thing, and deeper enlightenment. My wife, always a powerful force, drove the effort and was fully supported. It was decided that we would all read the book *Stamped: Racism, Antiracism, and You: A Remix of the National Book Award-winning Stamped from the Beginning* by Jason Reynolds and Ibram X. Kendi. And we would read it together. And not just read it, but discuss it together, share ideas and insights, perspectives and personal feelings, and do it in a safe space. And we did.

From my own personal perspective, the book had an excellent historical base. The facts and what followed from there were clear and straightforward. There were many "ah ha" and "I didn't know that" moments. It was also written in a way that was highly engaging, and continuously clever. It was a very good read with multiple solid messages.

However, as we went on, I found the messages to be less historically based, and more and more opinionated. To this, I found myself straying further from some of the messaging (and conclusions). And there were parts of the book that I just completely disagreed with, and quite frankly found somewhat insulting. I decided to take what I could from what I learned via the authors' research, and leave the rest behind.

The discussions with the family, as we read, on the other hand, were truly priceless. Some perspectives were very similar to my own, and some simply were not. To hear my children share their views and thoughts was both impressive and encouraging. These young souls had true truths to express, and I was even prouder than expected. When we disagreed, it was handled well, for the most part. Sometimes the back and forth when folks saw things differently got a little heated, but never out of hand. In fact, it was often that when differences of opinion arose, it was a few on one side and a few on the other. And sometimes, a few on a third side as well! However, we would look for common ground and understanding, and usually found it.

It was during these shared readings that I would find myself saying things like "And when they brought us here in chains…" or "We were forced to live like…" or "We had to fight for our lives and our freedom…" or "Even after slavery was over, they still treated us like…" and on and on and on I continued. I was very much into the book and everything that I was sharing. That went without question. But something was off, just not quite right. I kept saying "we" and "us" and "our." I know for sure that my family knew that I meant we, us, and our as a shared experience from those that came before. Our ancestors. But the thing is that those people that I was referring to were not *my* ancestors. Not really, no. As my family knows, and from what I shared in my first book, *Welcome Home*, I was not born here in America. We arrived here on December 12, 1972, at JFK Airport in New York City. And my journey to citizenship was a complicated and challenging venture (y'all gotta read that book!). So, my ancestors were not from here. They were not captured from their land and homes, taken from their country, put into bondage. They were not slaves in America. The more that I used the "we" and "us" and "our" phrases, the stranger it felt (and internally sounded). The more I professed the struggle of "our people," the more distant I perceived it. It was like I was expressing another person's experiences and emotions. It was more than just strange. I began to feel disingenuous, almost phony or false.

I don't believe that this was fully lost on my family. At one point, it was somewhat stated that although we (my family) came directly from Africa (Nigeria, etc.), it's possible that I might have had relatives who were captured too, brought to this country, and sold into slavery. This is entirely possible and would indeed provide the connective tissue that linked me to slavery, or at least a potential family member. Done! But that at best would be a distant relation. Very distant. And that would not address the fact that no one in my direct line would trace back to American slavery. No one.

As a matter of fact, prior to our shared readings, my older brother, a long time ago, had already conveyed that he could (and did) trace our paternal lineage back several generations, literally hundreds of years back, and all right in Nigeria. How was I to express the anger or passion or sorrow or pain of someone who was not directly from that time and even place, through my ancestors? I started to use the phrases less and less as we went forward. And the feelings never left.

# CHAPTER 9

When we had completed our shared readings, I found myself reflecting on this more and more. It eventually weighed on me heavily. Who was I? Both of my parents are Nigerian, as are theirs, and thus so are my ancestors. And theirs as well. Yet, I was born in the country of Gabon, in the city of Libreville. Indeed, at the time of this writing, I have never stepped foot on Nigerian soil. We traveled from country to country, continent to continent, and eventually ended up in America (again in 1972). And for years, we, I was a permanent resident. And in 2012, I finally became a US citizen (all in the first book people). So, again, what did that make me? Perhaps this is why there always seemed to be an internal struggle within me regarding my identity, and trying to figure it out, and what it all made me. I let this sink into me and really take root. In those days and weeks and months that followed our shared readings, and the years since my father's passing, and since becoming a US citizen, I turned inwards and let myself explore the depths of my soul and my perceived misalignment to answer that very question.

I found myself going very far back, all the way to when I was in early elementary school. I recall how different I was than the other children in school and the neighborhood, and that I really didn't want to be. Truth be told, I feel that most kids don't want to be different, but just want to fit right in, and be pretty much like everyone else, at least at that age, around five or six years old. I don't mean different like having a unique style, or having a "cool" gift (run faster or jump higher than others). I just mean being seen as "different." My family was not from California or New York. We were from Africa. It doesn't get much more different than that. My mother would always tell me that Libreville was a French city. The official language there was French. I did not know that it was because it was colonized by the French, and that they controlled it until 1960. She would always tell me that since I was born there, I was a Frenchman. Clearly, I now understand what she meant, but back then my very young mind somehow warped that into me "being" from France. And then in short order, being "born" in the city of Libreville, in France. I'm still not sure where that leap came from, or looking back now, how that was any less different, but it did sound pretty cool, and more so it sounded true. I was born in Libreville, a French place. I was a Frenchman. Thus, I was born in France. Done! I wasn't asked too often about where I was from. I believe that for the most part, all the other kids just thought that I was a tall Black kid. I really didn't speak with any type of accent or drawl (thanks to my mother teaching us all English before we started school).

So, besides my appearance, I generally fit in, or so I thought.

I recall vividly back when I was in the 2nd grade, one morning while waiting for the bus, that there was another kid picking on a friend of mine. I went over to them (they were a little ways off), took my friend by the arm and pulled him away from the other kid, putting myself between the two of them. The bullying kid stopped and looked at me for a few moments. I didn't say a word and just let my size speak for me, looking directly at him. He looked back at me and after a short while he said it. "Nigger." At first, I just stood there, staring. In all honesty I didn't know quite how to respond. So, I stared. He didn't say anything else. I eventually turned and walked away. I showed no reaction to it, no emotion, not a hint of anything. But I did feel it. There was a sting. I knew the word. But I wasn't sure exactly what I should do. I had heard it on TV when we were encouraged (more like made) to watch the television series "Roots." I had heard it around school (although there were very few folks who looked like me at school). But no one had ever called me that before. As I walked away back then, I didn't know how to process what I was feeling. And eventually, actually quite quickly, it went away. I do recall thinking that the kid never took a step toward me, or even moved in my direction at all. He was pushing and shoving my friend freely, but with me, except for one word, nothing. That stuck with me too.

This was Vermont back in the 1970s. Identity was always present, but very rarely brought up.

We eventually moved to Arizona from Vermont. And in the early 80s, when I was in the 6th grade, our teacher Mr. Luke was assigning us projects that had to do with our backgrounds, where we were from, born, etc. He was asking if we knew, and for us to share it with the class. I heard kids say Texas, Arizona, New Mexico, and on and on. Even Alaska. When he got to me, I said that I was born in France. A few kids chuckled because I think that was a little different. Mr. Luke said that that didn't sound right to him, and that he was going to check. He actually went over to his desk, opened a drawer, and pulled out a file. Yes, an actual file with my (and I assume the rest of the class's as well) records in it. I watched closely as he opened it up. He took a moment and then said, "You were born in Libreville. In Gabon." The class was quiet. Then he said, "That's in Africa." Then the class erupted in laughter. I just stared, knowing that he was wrong. He then shouted at the class to be quiet, and that there was nothing wrong with that. The class calmed down. I saw that most of them were looking at me, just staring. As I looked back around at them, in that moment I felt strange, and embarrassed. And different. He was wrong. Just wrong. Mr. Luke went on to the next kid. The moment passed and that was it. No one made fun of me. There were no jokes later. Nobody said a word that day, or the next, or the next. Things just continued. But I'll never forget it. Ever. I even remember where I was sitting in the class, the blue shirt that Mr. Luke was wearing at the time. And the laughter.

In the mid-80s, after my first year of high school, we moved to Florida. That was a huge change. When we started school, I had never seen so many African American kids in my life. It was, on the one hand, somewhat stunning. There were as many differences within the race as there were between races. It took some time to get used to. On the other hand, I didn't seem quite so different, which felt pretty good, at least to a degree. I was still well over six feet tall, with a somewhat lighter skin tone, and bright green eyes. Because of this, and perhaps my speech pattern (a whole lot of the Black kids spoke with more of an urban accent), I was asked if I was mixed. Mixed? Or if one of my parents was White. White? Really? If they only knew. I was called a redbone (What?? First time I heard that), and even "yellow"! Again, really? These questions and comments, to be fair, were very few and very far between, extremely rare. But they were none the less posed. I usually or normally answered no, or just ignored it. Hearing this from other Black folks "exposed" me to a whole new type of "different" and shifted my focus of trying to fit in. If the White kids saw me as obviously different, for very obvious reasons, and the Black kids (at least a small few) saw me as different for other reasons, then what was the point of trying so hard to fit in? Really? People would either accept me, or they would not. It took me some time to figure all of this out. In the meantime, I played sports, and got better and better. I studied hard, and got smarter and smarter. And I made acquaintances, buddies, teammates, and friends. Boys and girls. These people who I knew, and who knew me made things much easier. The myriad of differences that I witnessed were not something to be shuttered or diminished. They were meant to be observed and honored. Race and all. As I felt more comfortable around my surroundings, I felt more comfortable about myself. My achievements were based on my actions. My accomplishments were due to my hard work. Nothing and everything reflected my differences. And nothing and everything depended on it too. My differences were what made me who I was, and I grew to really like that. And so did the folks that I kept close. My friends were as eclectic as my environment. And they were extremely welcoming and accepting, regardless. Truly regardless. With this acceptance came more freedom. It didn't matter who I hung out with, or for the most part what we did. I found myself searching, finding, changing, and rediscovering my own style. My own sense of self. On my own terms, as I saw fit. Fitting in was not a factor anymore. Truth be told, standing out became a pursuit, again to a degree.

Over time, I found that I leaned into this more and more. The only thing that stayed the same was the fact that things changed. And they did. And I did too. The process was somewhat slow, but it did happen.

By my senior year, I had faced, and I feel, conquered my issues with this. There were some truly "ah ha" moments. However, I found that as time passed, and I lived my day-to-day, sometimes as mundane as that could be, I had changed. Much more than just physically, but also mentally, emotionally, and spiritually. I had altered my perception of who I was, perhaps intentionally or unintentionally, and that led to an evolution of self. A true transformation, sometimes much too subtle to perceive. This did not take place overnight, or in one specific jaw-dropping, eye-opening, epiphany-driven moment. No. It was gradual and granular, which sometimes is the essence of change.

I contribute that to certain folks and friends. I contribute that to the time spent with each of them. These individuals from different friend groups, some individually, some a part of a greater number, all added to my sum total being more than the individual pieces and parts that made me who I was. I attribute that to their patience, and openness. I contribute that to their warmth and compassion. I attribute that to their seeking and searching in both the ways that I was, and the ways that I wasn't. We were all looking for something, in our own way, on our own terms, for our own selves. Some of these folks and friends mostly didn't cross paths with each other. As far as I knew, some of them didn't really know each other at all. But they all knew me, and I got to know them, some better than others. But these folks and friends, whether accidentally or by design, held me up and moved me forward. And for that I thank them.

As an 18th birthday present for myself, I had asked my family for a gold onyx ring, an onyx stone in a gold band and setting. This to me represented myself as that strong Black gem encased in the most precious metal of gold. I took it as a celebration of my value and worth as a Black man. And as a symbol of never doubting that worth. Ever. And for all to finally see it too. I got that ring for my birthday, and it was a proud moment. I wore it on my left ring finger, a place of prominence and prestige. I only moved it to my right ring finger when I got married, over a decade later. Tragically it was stolen from my car several years later. Long story. I'm still disappointed and saddened by the loss to this day. But more on that to come.

# CHAPTER 10

As I continued to reflect, and while on my path of, and to, self-discovery, again after our shared readings of the *Stamped* book, I came to realize that while my struggles of differences were resolved regarding race, this was not the case regarding ethnicity or origin. Yes, of course, I was Black and from another country, but again, who was I?

I thought back again to high school, and the Black kids that I got to know. So many of them traced their linage back to the beginnings of this country. Interestingly, many of them had parents and grandparents who all attended this exact same school that we were attending then as well. When these kids spoke, or when their parents whom I met spoke, the speech patterns were the same, which was so ironic given that my father spoke with a very thick accent, and my mom had a very slight one too, but I had none. None of my siblings did. I was even accused of "talking White" on multiple occasions, by multiple people. These African American friends of mine could share stories that went back generations and took place right here. They could talk about their parents and grandparents moving from state to state, not country to country, or continent to continent. They're the ones who could use the "we" and "us" and "our" with full legitimacy, full ownership, full truth. They knew where their ancestors migrated to in this country, where they came from. They knew who they were.

But in high school, I also saw another side of things. In South Florida, at least back then, and even now, there was a large population of Haitians. This was just as true in my high school. I recall when I took French I and French II, there was a large contingent of them in these classes. And I believe that most, if not all of them spoke Creole as a first language. They had thick accents, and our teacher conversed fluently with them in French. These kids were clearly from somewhere else. They had different styles of clothes, mannerisms, and speech. They interacted mainly with each other and didn't seem to care about what others knew, or what others thought. They did their thing, loud and proud, judger be damned. I must admit, that did come across to me as somewhat bold. While my own style was more reserved and reflective, they seemed to celebrate their history and culture in a big and open way. That both intrigued and impressed me. While being as "loud" as some of them were was not my way (let me stress SOME of them, not all), and under some situations, I found it a little embarrassing for them yelling down the hall in Creole or speaking very fast and at a higher than average volume to each other, while standing right next to each other (seriously, right next to each other!!), I came to realize that there was a strength in not holding back, not acclimating, not confirming. This stuck with me then, and still does now. I don't think that I could have done that, conducted myself that way back then. Perhaps it was just not in my nature, regardless. But there they were. There it was, whatever it was. They had it and lived it. Again, strength.

As I reflected more on this, just this, I began to realize that this quietness could be more akin to culture. This reserve could be a product, or indeed a staple of how we were raised. In our house growing up there was a tremendous amount of talk, and banter and laughing and telling and sharing, and such. The communication flowed easily and effortlessly. This was most especially true around the dinner table. Main conversations would ebb and flow in several different directions with everyone welcome to share. This manner of conversation continued into my adulthood and to my own family table and household. In fact, this is still present when we attend holiday gatherings at my family's houses. Free open flowing outpourings of thoughts and expressions, and opinions and perspectives. All with much laughter and love.

However, as children we were raised with strict manners, and that included respect for our elders, and family. When it was time for a serious discussion, then that's what occurred, along with all the trappings that came with it. And when we went out together, especially together, proper manners were paramount, and good behavior was more than expected, it was required. I never felt that it was a weight or burden. It was as natural as breathing. In fact, to see other kids act up and out was actually disturbing. Centuries later, when I was raising children of my own, that mindset presented a challenge. However, over time, I came to realize that these acts of rebellion or defiance were methods and sources of growth and learning, both for them, my children, and me. Strength also flows from patience, and patience takes strength. So, perhaps that Nigerian culture of respect and proper behavior instilled in me a quiet reserve. Perhaps it aided me in skills of discipline and thoughtfulness. But what else might it have pushed down in me, and to what degree? I'm just not sure.

At this point in my reflections, I feel that it is of paramount importance that I make one thing perfectly clear. While I have been going on and on about the kids (and some adults) that I encountered, by no means do I think, feel or believe that they were all of the same type. Not at all. There were plenty of kids who shared my hue (or race) that spoke just as similar as each other, or me. And there were those who spoke, or dressed, or carried themselves just as differently as each other, or me. We were all different from each other, and anyone, everyone else. I saw no stereotypes or typical anything's or anyone's. All different, all of us.

My high school days were very consistent regarding my identity. I didn't focus too much on it. There was so much going on, so much happening at that time, that my main priorities were academics, athletics, social situations, and whatever was going on at home. In my book *Welcome Home*, I go a little deeper into that (my home situation) specifically. I do recall being asked about where I was from on occasion, given my unique look and very interesting (some might say unusual (and I've heard it called strange)) last name. "Ezeilo" was not usual in any way, shape, or form. I replied in the manner that I had trained myself to respond, "My parents are from Nigeria." Nigeria??!! was the usual response, typically followed by a perplexed look, or an "Oh really," or a surprised gaze, or sometimes even a joke or smart comment. And I found myself normally not going too much further until or unless specifically asked. A few folks found it very interesting. Again, typically, I offered more only when asked. As aforementioned, consistent.

Through more reflection, I realized that my college days were somewhat similar. I will admit that I did encounter a much more diverse group of people. And more mature as well. I found myself offering more details as I met more folks. For the ones that I got close to, I found that I easily expressed more and more of who I was, and where I was from. I felt an ease and comfort. And a true sincere interest. But there was still a general guarding, a relaxed reserve. I noticed that this continued throughout my college career. I truly feel that this was, and is, just my nature. I prefer to be more quiet and listening, more reserved and still. Please do not get it wrong. I am fully capable of being a large part of, or indeed, the full-blown life of the party. I love all things silly, enjoy both making folks smile, and smiling myself, etc. That goes for laughing too. Easily. Instinctively. Joyously. So perhaps opening up and sharing with the right people, regardless of the topics, was just natural.

However, even with that being the case, my priorities were not my identity. Not then. My focus on race did materially increase. This was due not only to my present environment, but to the larger national and global environment as well. There seemed to be a greater emphasis and concentration on the Black experience, Black culture, Black society, and Black excellence. Things were changing. And while wearing my onyx ring in its gold setting, I absorbed and marveled at this change too. Whether through casual or serious discussions, or dating, or being honored with an award for an MLK scholarship or SECME award and scholarship, it was everywhere. It easily overshadowed anything identity-related. Race, being Black, a Black man, mattered more.

As I reflect on this now, I see how utterly insane that line of thinking was. And still is. What could I have possibly been thinking? Here (back then) I was, a young man, a young Black man, a young Black man with direct roots to Africa, Nigeria, Igbo people, and I didn't lean into that. How? Goodness, how? I was so focused on just being Black that the heritage of that attribute did not connect. Wait. Correction. I was so focused on just being Black *in America*, that the heritage of that attribute did not connect. It was more the Black man's plight in this country that caught my mindset. There, here and now. More so, and unfortunately, it was the history of the Black race in this country that was the main topic, the central issue, the primary concern. In a very real way that made sense. After all that was the majority of the Black folks' shared experience. Generations of pain and suffering, of grief and despair, of loss. It was the years and decades and centuries of subhuman treatment. It was the lingering perception of "less than" and "not worthy" that remained. And remains. All of this and so much more was easy to attach to. And I did. And in doing so, I readily attached to all of it. How could I not? Race was bigger than identity. How unfortunate my thinking was. It was narrow, and small, and short-sided, and off, and again truly unfortunate.

My college years turned into my professional years. And I continued. During interviews, I was asked to talk about myself. I almost always began with, "My parents were from Nigeria." In actuality, I found that this intro worked pretty well. Interviewers always seemed to perk up and take a little greater interest. I would then follow it up with, "and we came to this country when I was two years old." That kind of rounded it out for them, but also subtly stated that I grew up here, right here, in the US of A. I would also state the same verbiage to colleagues and coworkers. It was true, but somewhat skewed. I got comfortable communicating this. It was easy, and I had much experience.

Following our shared readings, my thoughts began to change. They morphed into something just not being right. About a lot of things. Shared struggles over hundreds of years? "We", "us", "our"? Hhmmmm. I'm an American now, right? Why shouldn't or couldn't I say or think these words or thoughts? Things were just not as clear-cut as they once were. Things were off.

These thoughts persisted. I attributed it to being raised here since I was two years old. I had started to see myself as those kids in high school who had been here for generations, and I later identified with my expanded environment in college. This persisted. Although I never forgot where I came from (read *Welcome Home* for way more details friends), I just didn't let it overshadow my race overall, if that makes sense. It didn't.

It doesn't. It just doesn't. Not anymore. Not after everything that had happened up to that point. Internally and externally. I sat with this confusion for a long time. Far too long. I let my conscience take me where it led. Wherever that was. And finally, after far too long, I arrived.

# CHAPTER 11

I believe, upon reflection, true reflection and introspection, that I understood. Really felt and understood. My race. My heritage and lineage. All of it was my identity. Together. Fully meshed. Inseparable. Complete. Truth be told, I knew this. I knew it fully and for a very, very long time. However, I had been so focused on one and not the other. I was so preoccupied with how I appeared and not where I had originated. So fixed on not being so different, indeed too different, that I gave so little attention to something that meant so much. In fact, I realized that it was my heritage that truly defined me. Just as it was also my race. And my faith. And my values. And my reflections. And my intentions. And on and on. And so much more. And me. There it was! At last, there it was! The imbalance that I had felt deep down, that I had pressed deep down. There it was.

Throughout much of my past, and indeed this writing, I had been using the word identity incorrectly. Just plain wrong. I had been one-sided and sloppy. I had been ignorant. And dumb. Identity may mean many things to many people. Simply put, it is what characterizes us, our individuality. At least that is what it means to me, in the simplest, broadest form. One can identify as just about anything: multiple things: straight, gay, bi, Black, White, person of color, Christian, Jew, Muslim, feminist, activist, SJW, liberal, conservative, independent, etc., etc., etc. It just depends on how they see themselves, and their individual unique incredible story.

I realized that there was a uniqueness to my story that didn't begin with me. I realized that there was a line of ancestors, on both sides, that significantly made me who I was. Who I am. I realized that those lines contributed to my family in a major way. My fathers and mothers, my brothers and sisters, my sons and daughter. I realized that I could not look at those that I loved so much, held so dear, and not be grateful. I realized that my parents sacrifices and strength, their love and protection, their dedication and commitment needed to be honored. And while I did indeed honor the people, the two of them, I did not do so fully. I did not take into consideration where they came from as it relates to what made them who and what they were. Perhaps this might be because of how and why we left. When my parents fled Nigeria at the end of the war (full details in *Welcome Home*, keep up), my mother was pregnant with me. Again, I was not even born there. I feel, unfortunately, that much of my connection with my past, my heritage, my roots, my people, was lost. But it was never truly forgotten. Quite the contrary. Throughout my life, as we went from country to country, from continent to continent, from state to state, and from city to city, those connections were ever-present. They were there in our family routines, through worship and respect. They were there in our family traditions, from speeches at special occasions, to Nigerian blessings at my wedding. They were there in the way that the adults dressed, in traditional robes and head garments during special events (still do, and so to do members of the next generation). They were there when we were told stories of where we came from – how water was fetched, and items were carried on the heads of women. They were there in the telling of our fables and tales – including about a character called Godim Jim (I hope that I spelled that right - he was a kind of folklore boogeyman that you would not want to encounter, dressed in nothing (*nothing*!) but a chain around his waist that was tied to a tire (Yeah!), so behave, kids!!). They were there in the music that almost always echoed from our family stereo throughout the house on the weekends. I still recall listening to Fela Kuti, a Nigerian musician, bandleader, and composer (and no doubt where I got my love of jazz, absolutely no doubt). He was known and widely regarded as the creator of Afrobeat, which is a Nigerian genre that combined Western African music with American jazz and even funk. As this music played during my childhood, I remember watching my father dance to the song *Shakara*. And I remember my mother singing the song *Lady* (I still listen to this music often when I'm on the treadmill, very often). They were there in the descriptions, actions, professional and personal lives of our cousins, and uncles and aunts, and our grandfathers and grandmothers. I personally love how my mother would speak about how my grandfather on my father's side, James, would make fun of my grandfather on my mother's side, her father Samuel being too good-looking. Grandfather James would say that he doesn't trust anyone that good-looking! Jokingly of course. And she would talk about how both of my grandfathers got along so very well. Apparently, I got my height, skin tone, and green eyes from her father. And my mother would also share how she did **NOT** get along with her mother-in-law. I believe that the phrase that she used was, "She used to traumatize me, and put me through…". Classic. I absolutely love talking to my mother about things and people from back then and back there. Love it.

I also vividly recall listening intently and engagingly as my father shared stories of the Biafran War with me. He was a high-ranking officer (I've been told that he was a lieutenant colonel, and read that he was a general), and head of the Biafran Airforce. I remember the pain in his voice as he took me through his memories and experiences of that time. One of these included his recounting to me a specific mission that he flew and led. It was successful. However, on the way back they were shot down. After the plane crash-landed, my father shared the events that followed, which included watching and hearing his copilot suffer and die, as his body had been severed and split open during the crash, and he was calling out to my father, who was trapped, for help. They fought for what they believed in and sacrificed greatly for it. I believe that I saw and felt his pride and grief at the same time. I rarely asked questions or sought more details. But I was very much taken back to that time, and better understood the man, this man, my father, because of it.

When my mother spoke of her father, she would smile. Always. She described him as a "great, great father." And talked about him fondly. She spoke about family trips at different times of the year, and her experiences. She also shared about the loss of her sister at a young age. The pain was clear and present.

I recall my mother sharing a story about my father's birth (I've shared this on social media). In 1938, in the city of Enugu, Nigeria, my father was born. He was part of a set, a pair, a twin. He and my aunt shared this special day. Fun fact, when they were born, back then, back there, it was believed that people were born individually. Being born a twin was considered a curse, and only reserved for cats and goats (no kidding, goats!!)! Needless to say, they were ostracized. After a couple of years of this, my grandmother took those two, and all of her children at the time, to their home village where that mindset persisted, and proudly displayed her twins. At first people fled, gripped with fear (yeah, actual fear). She stood strong. They ran and screamed. She stood strong. They would not look. She stood strong and proud. After some time, folks came back, examined the pair (oh no they didn't - oh yes, they did!!), and finally, fully accepted them. This was the beginning of his beginning.

My mother also shared that my father wanted to join the seminary and become a priest. Back then, back there, you needed both parents' permission to do so. His father supported it and gave his blessing. His mother did not. So, he eventually entered the military, flew jets, fought in a civil war, and fled the country of his birth and lineage, with a young family in tow. All this before I was born.

I remember so many other details of practices and tradition that resonated throughout my upbringing. These included the special meals, with large helpings of Nigerian jollof rice, that we shared after church on Saturday evenings, based on cooking that began hours earlier. These also included nightly prayers as a family, together, on our knees, in our living room, beginning with the Lord's Prayer, other prayers, and eventually our own individual intercessions, and ending with a prayer song, sung in our native language of Igbo. Looking back now, I see how beautiful that was. Every night. These were bestowed on me, on us, by our parents. There was a very real infusion of who we were as Nigerians in so very many things that we experienced and were exposed to. My mother and father created this weaving together of cultures, and I see now that this tapestry has helped me significantly in the development of my identity.

As I continued to reflect on this, I truly realized that these two people, my parents, were themselves of their own lines. These lines, patriarchal and matriarchal extended back farther than even they knew, and pulled forward through time, through them, through us, through me, and forward still. Their history is my history. This is where I am from. It awesomely dawned on me that these lines, back through time and forward moving, everlastingly, is who I am. I let this drape over me, and cover me completely, from the outside to within. I began to feel a shift and then an alignment, as I absorbed it all. And with this revelation comes satisfaction and comfort. And as I continued to reflect, and adjust, I felt something else. I felt a shameless heavy pride. This is who I am. How can I feel otherwise? This feels right to me. To honor my history beyond me; to honor my heritage, truly. To take pride in my line. This feels right.

My wife bought a book called *Surviving Biafra, The Story of the Nigerian Civil War* by Alfred Uzokwe. The book chronicles the author's family's account of the Biafran War just before, during and after the war. At the time of the war, he was eight years old. He was from the Igbo people, just like my family (and on the same side). Members of his family fought in the war, just like my family. There was pride in the new young country of Biafra in his family, just like my family. And although I was not born until near the very end of the war, reading his accounts of what occurred both before and during the conflict mirrored so much of what had been shared with me by my parents about their homes, our home, our country, back then, back there. The more that I read, the more that I both learned and strangely and wonderfully remembered, even though I was not born at the time. Memories of what had been shared with me much later, were experienced in that book. The traditions from the pages that were carried forward through my childhood and beyond. The customs from his stories that were present in my family, my home. The culture from his words that were a bedrock of my everyday existence. Through his book I found an even deeper connection to my own past, people, place and self. And from there, more pride. Alfred Uzokwe, I thank you. Very much.

# CHAPTER 12

So, through my reverie and reflection, on my journey of self-discovery and identity, where am I now? What have I learned? I am here to be seen now, and have learned much. First of all, I believe that I best describe myself, among other things, as am immigrant son of immigrant parents. I feel in this space that this presents the most accurate and complete picture of who I am. To say only that my parents are immigrants totally excludes me from that summary. To say that I am an immigrant excludes them from the same summary, as one can assume that I have come here without them. To say that "we" are immigrants would be accurate, but in some way incomplete. To me, this does not accentuate the distinction of my parents' duel experiences, both in their native Nigeria and in America, as well as my almost full life here in the US, and the uniqueness and intrigue of the merged cultures of my almost entire upbringing. Immigrant son of immigrant parents speaks to it all.

Additionally, and very importantly, in this understanding of identity, as I look back through my childhood and forward, I also realized that as an African American, or any Black person here in America, while we might not have been born here, we are indeed *of* here. It did not matter if you were just arriving from elsewhere or if your ancestors had been here for hundreds of years. If you were Black, you would be subject to the same stigmas, stereotypes, harassment and hostilities regardless. As great as this country is, and as much as it has grown and evolved, there is still a long way to go regarding racial equality, bias and perspective.

This vast gap is backed by facts and data. Looking at recent details from the Bureau of Labor and Statistics, October 2023, regarding earnings and employment, Blacks earn 81% of what Whites earn. For employment, using the employment-population ratio, which is the proportion of the population that is employed, for adult males over 20 years old, for Whites it is 58.6%, and for Blacks it is 55.7%. Also, according to the Institute of Education Sciences (IES), which is the statistics, research, and evaluation arm of the U.S. Department of Education, regarding high school graduation rates as measured by the adjusted cohort graduation rate (ACGR), in 2019–20, the ACGRs for Blacks was 81 percent for public high school students, which was below the U.S. average ACGR of 87 percent. While the ACGRs for Whites was 90 percent. Regarding college, the percentage of bachelor's degrees conferred by postsecondary institutions in 2020-21 for Black males was at 8.9% and for Black females was at 11.6%, while for White males and females it was at 61.9% and 58.2% respectively.

Regarding health, according to the US Census Bureau in 2021, Black adults had significantly higher levels than White adults of arthritis, diabetes and hypertension. Hypertension was about three times as common among Black adults than White adults. And according to the National Institutes of Health, in 2019, overall life expectancy was 78.9 years for Whites and 75.3 years for Blacks.

Let's keep going, and just summarize from here:

**Wealth Gap**

- **Statistic**: In 2019, the median wealth of White households was $188,200, compared to $24,100 for Black households.

- **Source**: *Federal Reserve, "Survey of Consumer Finances" (2019).*

**Income Inequality**

- **Statistic**: In 2022, the median household income for White households was about $81,000, while for Black households, it was around $52,000.

- **Source**: *U.S. Census Bureau, "Current Population Survey" (2022).*

**Homeownership**

- **Statistic**: As of 2023, the homeownership rate for White Americans was 74.5%, while for Black Americans, it was 44.9%.

- **Source**: *U.S. Census Bureau, "Housing Vacancies and Homeownership" (2023).*

## Unemployment Rate

- **Statistic**: As of August 2023, the unemployment rate for Black Americans was 6.6%, compared to 3.3% for White Americans.

- **Source**: *U.S. Bureau of Labor Statistics, "Employment Situation Summary" (August 2023).*

## Poverty Rate

- **Statistic**: In 2021, about 19.5% of Black Americans lived in poverty, compared to 8.2% of White Americans.

- **Source**: *U.S. Census Bureau, "Income and Poverty in the United States" (2021).*

## Health Disparities

- **Infant Mortality Rate**: Black infants in the U.S. die at a rate of 10.8 per 1,000 live births, compared to 4.6 per 1,000 for White infants.

- **Source**: *Centers for Disease Control and Prevention (CDC), "National Vital Statistics Reports" (2021).*

- **Life Expectancy**: In 2021, the life expectancy for Black Americans was 71 years, compared to 76 years for White Americans.

- **Source**: *CDC, "National Center for Health Statistics" (2021).*

## Educational Attainment

- **Statistic**: As of 2022, 36% of White adults over 25 had a bachelor's degree or higher, compared to 26% of Black adults.

- **Source**: *U.S. Census Bureau, "Educational Attainment in the United States" (2022).*

## Incarceration Rates

- **Statistic**: Black Americans are incarcerated at a rate of 1,096 per 100,000, compared to 214 per 100,000 for White Americans. Black men are about 5.8 times more likely to be incarcerated than White men.

- **Source**: *The Sentencing Project, "Report on Incarceration Rates by Race" (2023).*

## Health Insurance Coverage

- **Statistic**: As of 2022, 11.8% of Black Americans were uninsured, compared to 7.5% of White Americans.

- **Source**: *U.S. Census Bureau, "Health Insurance Coverage in the United States" (2022).*

## Home Loan Approval Rates

- **Statistic**: In 2022, Black applicants were denied home loans at a rate of 20.8%, compared to a denial rate of 10.7% for White applicants.

- **Source**: *Consumer Financial Protection Bureau (CFPB), "Mortgage Market Activity and Trends" (2022).*

## Student Loan Debt

- **Statistic**: On average, Black college graduates owe $25,000 more in student loan debt than White college graduates four years after graduation.

- **Source**: *Brookings Institution, "Black-White Disparity in Student Loan Debt" (2016).*

## Health Outcomes: Hypertension

- **Statistic**: 57.1% of Black adults have hypertension, compared to 43.6% of White adults.

- **Source**: *American Heart Association, "Hypertension Prevalence and Control" (2021).*

## Maternal Mortality

- **Statistic**: Black women in the U.S. are more than three times as likely to die from pregnancy-related causes than White women.

- **Source**: *Centers for Disease Control and Prevention (CDC), "Pregnancy Mortality Surveillance System" (2021).*

## Life Expectancy Disparity During COVID-19

- **Statistic**: During the COVID-19 pandemic, the life expectancy for Black Americans dropped by 2.9 years, compared to a 1.2-year decrease for White Americans.

- **Source**: *National Center for Health Statistics (NCHS), "Provisional Life Expectancy Estimates" (2021).*

## Home Value Appreciation

- **Statistic**: Between 2004 and 2019, homes in predominantly Black neighborhoods appreciated 52% less than those in White neighborhoods.

- **Source**: *Brookings Institution, "The Devaluation of Assets in Black Neighborhoods" (2018).*

## Police Use of Force

- **Statistic**: Black Americans are 2.5 times more likely than White Americans to be killed by police.

- **Source**: *Proceedings of the National Academy of Sciences (PNAS), "Risk of Being Killed by Police Use of Force in the U.S. by Age, Race–Ethnicity, and Sex" (2019).*

## Employment Discrimination

- **Statistic**: Black applicants are 50% less likely than equally qualified White applicants to receive a callback or job offer.

- **Source**: *National Bureau of Economic Research (NBER), "Are Emily and Greg More Employable than Lakisha and Jamal?" (2003).*

## Food Insecurity

- **Statistic**: In 2021, 19.1% of Black households experienced food insecurity, compared to 7.1% of White households.

- **Source**: *U.S. Department of Agriculture (USDA), "Household Food Security in the United States" (2021).*

### Home Appraisal Bias

- **Statistic**: Homes in Black neighborhoods are often appraised for 23% less than similar homes in White neighborhoods.
- **Source**: *Brookings Institution, "The Devaluation of Assets in Black Neighborhoods" (2018).*

### Cancer Mortality Rates

- **Statistic**: The cancer mortality rate for Black Americans is 20% higher than for White Americans.
- **Source**: *American Cancer Society, "Cancer Facts & Figures for African Americans" (2022).*

These statistics further illustrate the persistent and wide-ranging disparities between Black and White Americans across various sectors, reflecting the undeniable and overt systemic inequalities.

The numbers do not lie.

We all have a ways to go. Whether you've been here for one generation or ten, it does not matter. We are all subject to everything from the so-called black tax to the perception that our lives matter less.

We're all *of* here now.

There are countless examples and a plethora of well-documented studies of the skewed disparities of the criminal justice system against Black folks in this country, including the disproportionate rates of incarceration.

Again, we're all *of* here now.

As a father myself, I had the joy of teaching each of my three sons how to drive. That joy was coupled with the unmistakable sadness of also teaching each of them the necessity of driving while Black. I really don't know what is sadder, the fact that I had to do the latter, or the fact that they each knew exactly what it was about and embraced it so completely.

Simply stated, we're all *of* here now.

And of course, there are the looks. The looks that some folks give others when they enter into a store, a gathering, or any public place, when those receiving the looks are perhaps younger, freer, browner, different, is a continued mark and symbol of where we are and how much further we have to go. I remember receiving those looks, long ago, and still. I recall the feelings then, when I received those looks, and how very much different the feelings are now. Very different. But the looks continue just the same.

We're all *of* here now.

Again, there has been much change and evolution in this country. And there are a myriad of wonderful people of all races who have, and continue to sacrifice for the uplifting and betterment of all. Those who recognize the faults and flaws of the past, and indeed the present and are willing to fight for change. Those whose hard work, dedication and commitment, blood, sweat, tears and lives, led to many firsts – the first Black president, first Black and female vice president, first Black Supreme Court Justice, etc. And those advances should be celebrated, to be sure. But there is still so much more work to do. While things are improving, the numbers do not lie. We are *of* here.

This knowledge and realization helped me reconcile the disconnects that I had while growing up, in schools, around others. Whether it was the kids whose families had been there for decades, or the newer kids, like the Haitians, fresh with their uniquely engaging accents and all, it made little difference. They, we, all had our origins from elsewhere. It just depended on how far back one was willing to go. But in the end, we were all there then, and here now together, looked at similarly, of this place. Trying to fit in, I believe, is a normal thing to do. However, the reasons why we feel that we are different, why we think that we stand out, are the real drivers. Those should be explored, yes, but then when identified and examined, be released. Or perhaps even celebrated. We're all different. And that is a very good thing.

# CHAPTER 13

It is at this point that I am taken elsewhere. I did not learn of this until much later in my life. However, on the same day that we arrived at JFK Airport, in New York City, on December 12th, 1972, as immigrants to this country, President Lyndon Baines Johnson (LBJ) was giving a Civil Rights Symposium address at the Lyndon Baines Johnson Library in Austin TX. Following is the exact speech:

*Mr. Middleton, esteemed former Chief Justice, and Miss Warren, and all of you wonderful people who have come here to try to make life better for your fellowmen:*

*I sat in the adjoining room and watched the panel this morning and got great satisfaction and compensation in my own way in feeling that all is not lost, all has not been in vain. All we have to do is kind of reorganize, reevaluate; and Rome wasn't built in a day and we can't overcome all the injustices or make this a perfect world overnight. But we are on our way in. We are going to do just that before it is over.*

*I don't speak very often or very long. My doctor admonished me not to speak at all this morning, but I'm going to do that because I have some things I want to say to you. I have a touch of sentimentality about me which has cost me a great deal in my 40 years in public life.*

*I say to all of you women, [uncertain at 2:05], Barbara Jordan, Yvonne Burke, and [uncertain at 2:09] and so many of you that I can't list them all, that it's natural for me to get a certain amount of glory by seeing the advances you are making and I guess it's just human for us to admire and be fond of the other sex, but when I listened in the adjoining room to Burke Marshall and Henry Gonzalez, Clarence Mitchell and Julian Bond whom I don't know so well but admire a great deal, I said to myself that I love these men more than a man ought to love another man, and that's my way of saying to you what great honor you do me by your presence and participation in these proceedings.*

*Of all the records that are housed in this library, 31 million papers over a 40-year period of public life, it is the record of this work that we have been discussing the last two days which had brought us here, that holds the most of myself within it and hold for me the most intimate meanings. In our system of government, honorable men honestly differ in their perceptions of government and what it's really all about, and today, I can speak only of my own perception, and I'm so proud I live in a government where I can do that.*

*I believe that the essence of government lies with unceasing concern for the welfare and dignity and decency and innate integrity of life for every individual. I don't like to say this and I wish I didn't have to add these words to make it clear, but I will: regardless of color, creed, ancestry, sex, or age.*

*Before I go any further, I want to interject, I'm so happy Miss Whitney Young is here. Her husband gave me great inspiration and leadership, and along with some of his colleagues, advanced these nation centuries in a decade. He is somewhere doing his good work today and it's in behalf of this fellow man, wherever he is.*

*I do not want to say that I've always seen this matter in terms of the special plight of the Black man as clearly as I came to see it in the course of my life and experience and responsibility. Now, let me make it plain that when I say black, as I do a good many times in this little statement, I also mean brown and yellow and red, and all other people who suffer discrimination because of their color or their heritage. Every group meets its own special problems, of course, but in a very broad sense, the problem of equal justice applies to us all.*

*Up on the second floor of this library in a special exhibit designed especially for this occasion, you will see the original Emancipation Proclamation by which our great President Abraham Lincoln ordered that the slaves should be freed of their bondage. A decade ago, in year 1963, we observed the 100th anniversary of that proclamation signing. On Memorial Day of that fateful year, I was called upon as the last President to speak at Gettysburg Cemetery where a century before, words had been spoken which all of us have long remembered, and on that occasion, I said this, until justice is blind to color, until education is unaware of race, until opportunity is unconcerned with the color of men's skin, emancipation will be a proclamation but not a fact. To the extent that the proclamation of emancipation is not fulfilled in fact, to that extent, we have fallen short of assuring freedom to the freed.*

*When I spoke those words as Vice President, I could not know that the future would present me shortly with the opportunity and the responsibility to contribute more toward fulfilling the fact of emancipation. Even if I could have known what lay ahead, I'm not sure now that I could have believed at that time that the progress, which has been won in these past 10 years, is a fact.*

*Black Americans are voting now, where they were not voting at all 10 years ago, but let me say quickly that not enough are voting. Little more than half of all eligible Americans voted in the last national election. I don't know how many of those that didn't vote were Black, but I do know this, we have to come up with some kind of plan or incentive to perfect our democracy by seeing that more of our people do vote and I certainly mean to include more of our Black people.*

*Now, I don't know how to do it. I don't want to get into it from the hip, with compulsory voting, but we ask our young men, we require them by law to all go and register for the draft. We require all of our children to go to school. We require our people, under the great laws of privilege, to have a Social Security Number. I have no doubt but what this would be a better country and a purer democracy if 95% of our people voted and the 5% that didn't had an exemption because of illness or whatever it might be, but when the hand of government reached out to them, if they had to reach in their purse or pocket book and show a stamp that they had voted, for the party of their choice and the individual of their choice, this would be a better land.*

*Black Americans are working now where they were not working 10 years ago. Black Americans, Brown Americans, Americans of every color and every condition are eating now and shopping now, going to the bathroom now and riding now, and spending nights now and obtaining credit now, and giving now, and attending classes now, going and coming in dignity were and as they were never able to do in years before.*

*I walked out of this room yesterday and looked at the sea of faces and I thought how proud Thurgood Marshall must be. I first met him when he came here on behalf of Herman Sweatt so a Black boy could come to the University of Texas and to look at this audience in this beautiful university auditorium, and see the groups that are participating today must make him feel and must make the groups that supported him feel that all has not been in vain.*

*But now that I've said that, I want to say this, I don't want this symposium to come here and spend two days talking about what we have done, the progress had been much too small. We haven't done nearly enough. I'm kind of ashamed of myself that I had six years and couldn't do more than I did. I'm sure all of you feel the same way about it.*

*I often tell the story about, that was reported and a fact about Churchill and the women's lib movement, maybe prohibition movement, a little ahead of our women over here, went into him after the war and said they were shocked to hear that if all the alcohol he consumed during the war, the brandy that he had drunk were emptied in the room, it would come up to about here.*

And Churchill looked on with a certain amount of satisfaction and amusement, instead of letting his feathers ride up. And he purported to have replied, "My dear little ladies, so little have I done, so much yet I have to do."

So, let no one delude themselves that our work is done. By unconcern, by neglect, by complacent beliefs that our labors in the field of human rights are completed, we of today can seed our future with storms that would rage over the lives of our children and our children's children. Yesterday, it was commonly said the Black problem was a southern problem. Today, it is commonly said that the Black problem is an urban problem – a problem of the inner city. But as I see it, the truth is that the Black problem today, as it was yesterday and yesteryear, is not a problem of regions or states or cities or neighborhoods. It is a problem, a concern, and responsibility of this whole nation.

Moreover, and we cannot obscure this one fact, the black problem remains what it has always been: the simple problem of being Black in a White society. And that is a problem, which our efforts have not yet been addressed. To be Black, I believe to one who is Black or Brown or what not is to be proud, is to be worthy, is to be honorable. But to be Black in a White society is not to stand on level and equal ground. While the races may stand side-by-side, Whites stand on history's mountain and Blacks stand in history's hollow. And until we overcome unequal history, we cannot overcome unequal opportunity.

That is not, nor will it ever be, a very easy goal for us to achieve. Individuals and groups who have struggled along to gain advantages for themselves do not readily yield the gains of their *struggles or their achievements so that others may have advantages or opportunities, but that is just the point now and always. There is no surrender, there is no loss involved, no advantage is safe, and no gain is secure in this society unless those advantages and those gains are opened up to all alike.*

*Where we have been concerned in the past for groups as groups, now we must become more concerned with individuals as individuals. As we have lifted the groups, the burdens of unequal law and custom, the next thrust of our effort must be to lift from individuals those burdens of unequal history. Not a White American in all this land would fail to be outraged if an opposing team tried to insert a 12th man in their football lineup to stop a Black fullback on the football field. Yet off the field, away from the stadium, outside of the reach of the television cameras, and the watching eyes of millions of their fellow men, every Black American in this land, man or woman, plays out life running against the 12th man of a history, that they did not make and a fate they did not choose.*

*In this challenge, our churches, our schools, our unions, our professions, our trades, our military, our private employers, and our government have a great duty from which they cannot turn. It is the duty of sustaining the momentum of this society's effort to equalize the history of some of our people so that we may open opportunity equally for all of our people.*

*Some may respond to these suggestions with exclamations of shock and dismay. Such proposals, they will say ask that special consideration be given to Black Americans rather than giving equal consideration to all Americans. I can only hear such protest through ears that are tuned by a lifetime to listening to the language of evasion. All that I hear now, I have heard before for 40 long years, in many forms and many forums. Give them the vote!*

*I saw a murder almost committed because I said that in 1937. Most people said, "unthinkable." Give them the right to sit wherever they wish on the bus. Impossible. Give them privilege of sitting at the same hotel, using the same restaurant, eating in the same counter, joining the same club, attending the same classroom. Never, never. Well, this crowd never I've heard since I was a little boy all my life. And what we commemorate on this great day is some of the work which has helped in some of the areas to make never now.*

*And I do not speak fulsomely. Most of that never would have been done without Burke Marshall, Roy Wilkins, Whitney Young, Chief Justice Warren, Julian Bond, all of those that are here today, Vernon Jordan. This never would have been done.*

*Now, here is what I want to say, what I have said is precisely the work which we must continue and this is a whole important part of this meeting – not all we have done, what we can do. So much, so little have we done. It oughtn't to take much place what we must do. So I think it's time to leave aside the legalisms and euphemisms and eloquent evasions. It's time we get down to business of trying to stand black and white on level ground.*

*For myself, I believe it's time for all of us in government and out to face up to the challenge. We must review and reevaluate what we have done and what we are doing. In specific areas, we must set new goals, new objectives, and new standards; not merely what we can do to try to keep things quiet, but what we must do to make things better. How much time will be given to that in this meeting? How much time we are going to give in the days ahead? How are we going to employ that? Who is going to bring our groups together? Who is going to select that leadership? What type of leadership are you going to do?*

*Specifically, I believe that we must direct our thought and efforts to many, many fields; and I don't have a great staff and little I can contribute in the way of leadership, but if I can leave the thought with those of you who do make up a great staff and who serve as my staff, I want to suggest a few little relatively unimportant thoughts as just some of the things to be put on your agenda. Are the federal government, the state government, the foundation and the churches, the university is doing what they can and all that they should to assure enough Black scholarships for young Blacks in every field? The answer is no. Very little.*

*It gets back to the same thing. Herman Sweatt can come to this university now, but as someone said on the panel this morning, Henry Gonzalez, I think, "What good is he doing sitting at the counter to get a cup of coffee if he doesn't have 50 cents to get it?" And most of them just don't have it. That's why they are not here. It's not their mother or their father who didn't want them here. It's not that they don't have an ambition to be here. They just can't do it and we've got to level out that ground son.*

*Or are professions such as law and medicine, accounting and engineering, and dentistry and architecture taking the initiative? Sounding the call to make certain that their educational programs are so planned and so conducted that Blacks are being prepared for the leadership courses and are being given the support that they must have if they are to complete the courses and to have genuine opportunities to establish themselves in positions of leadership, professional careers, and things of that matter after their college days.*

*Or are trade unions and all those concerned with vocational occupation doing the same to open up apprenticeships and training programs so that the Blacks, the group I spoke of, have a fair chance of entering and a fair chance of succeeding in these fields that are so vital to the future of our nation and to our country at this very moment?*

*Are our employers who have already made a start toward opening jobs to the Blacks doing what they can and should in order to make certain that Blacks qualify for advancement on the promotion ladder, and that the promotion ladder itself reaches out for the Blacks as it does for the others in our society?*

*What I'm saying is that we cannot take care of the goals to which we have committed ourselves simply by adopting a Black "star system." It is good and it is heartening and it is satisfying to see individual Blacks succeeding as stars in the field of politics, athletics, entertainment, and other activities where they have high visibility such as Clarence Mitchell referred to in his family. I felt almost as good in my own election -- not quite as good -- when Barbara and Yvonne were elected this year because I thought that we were moving forward and I enjoyed knowing of those elections about as much as I did in my own.*

*But we must not allow the visibility of a few to diminish the efforts to satisfy what is our real responsibility to the still unseen millions who are faced with that basic problem of being Black in a*

*White society. So our objective must be to assure that all Americans play by the same rules and all Americans play against the same odds. Who among us would claim that that is true today? I feel this is the first work of any society which aspires to greatness, so let's be on with it. We know there is injustice. We know there is intolerance. We know there is discrimination and hate and suspicion, and we know there is division among us. But there is a larger truth. We have proved that great progress is possible. We know how much still remains to be done.*

*And if our efforts continue, and if our will is strong, and if our hearts are right, and if courage remains our constant companion, then, my fellow Americans, I am confident we shall overcome.*

On the very same day that we arrived. Simply amazing.

That would be his last speech. He passed away 41 days later.

# CHAPTER 14

As I further reflect, and research, I am taken to immigrants who journeyed to this country and were arriving by the tens of thousands. For a forty-to-fifty-year period, between the late 1800's and the early 1900's there was a vast immigrant explosion into this country. My daughter was studying this in school and confirmed the facts, surprisingly. Millions poured into this country in that half-century timeframe. Millions in just under 50 short years.

In that span of time, approximately 23 to 27 million people immigrated to the United States. This period, often referred to as the "Great Wave" of immigration, saw a significant influx of people, particularly from Southern and Eastern Europe, including countries like Italy, Poland, and Russia. This wave also included immigrants from other regions, such as Asia and Scandinavia.

And they were welcomed, at least *into* the country by the government. Long lines, processing, some quarantined, etc. But they made it onto these shores and land. Free and legal. From there perhaps it was something else. I think about those poor huddled masses searching for a better life. And I wonder how so much has changed, at least in perception and attitude. To be sure, those people that came from other places, in that other time, were not all met with open arms. Quite the contrary in far too many cases. Signs like "XXX Not Welcome Here", or "YYY Need Not Appy" were part of the norm, and something that anyone just arriving had to face and needed to navigate. And they did. And kept coming. One factor in this is that many from other places had small, and sometimes not so-small, communities to welcome and support them. Whether it was a "Little XXX", or "YYY town", there were in essence "villages" to assist with that provided kinship, homecoming, and safety. Again, not for all, but for many.

I then began to wonder about those who had been here for decades and centuries. Ones who had no safe landing when they arrived. Ones who were taken by force and brought here unwillingly. What about them? And when battles were fought, and a nation was very nearly torn completely and irrevocably apart, and a war was finally won, or lost depending on which side you were on, what about them? What about their struggles?

At this point in time, I am reminded of people who look at these others, and say things like, "My family immigrated here from somewhere else, and we made it. We had nothing and we made it. We worked hard, and we made it. Why can't you? All those terrible things happened to you (or your people) so very long ago. It's in the past. All of it. There's nothing stopping you now. What's your excuse?"

I've heard all of these, and many more arguments before. To me it's an affront to the history of much of this country. It's a twisted and convoluted set of statements and questions, based on a tunnel-vision view of then and now. In the perhaps simplest explanation, truly simplest explanation, I can answer it like this.

A set of parents had two children. One child, resembling his parents, is very fair with bright, straight hair, and eyes that resemble the sea. The other child is a darker tone with strong short curly hair, and powerful eyes that look like the night sky. No resemblance at all. To the first child, they bestow all manner of favor upon him. They teach this child how to read and write. They indeed educate this child as much as possible. They take care of this child's every need, and satisfy his every want. They tell this child that he is special and wonderful, and that he can do and be anything that he wants to do and be. They work for this child, sacrifice for this child, protect this child, ensuring that he will receive his inheritance when the time comes, and they call it legacy and tradition. They tell this child that he is the best and greatest, over anyone else.

To the second child, they bestow no matter of favor on him, at all. They intentionally keep this child ignorant and provide no opportunity to read or write. They abuse this child in all manners and forms. They tell this child that he is useless (or dirty) and worthless. They tell this child that he will amount to nothing. They make this child work mercilessly for anything that he might receive. They tell this child that he is below everyone and everything else.

Then one day, while the caretakers are still providing, and protecting, and parenting the first child, they expel the second one, and let him fend for himself. At that significant moment, that specific point in time, how can there be any fraction of evenness? Any semblance of fairness? Any iota of balance between the two children? The first is not just in front of, or slightly before the second. He is light years ahead. Simply, light years ahead. The second is distantly behind, and is intentionally kept that way for far too long. Even with organizations erected to assist him, the damage done is deep and broad. And lasting. Poorer physical health, mental health, and emotional health; poorer quality of education, educational opportunities, educational advancements; poorer still economic conditions, higher poverty, fewer opportunities to build wealth. And on it continues.

And perhaps the worst of it all is the lasting perception. The mindset of just looking at the here and now, while ignorant of the past, and categorizing this second child (a whole class of people) as something negative, lower, not capable of. Maybe even unworthy, and mattering less than.

If one truly understood the enormity of what that second child had to endure and how far he has progressed, then one would marvel at the pure strength, character, and ability of this second son. Simply marvel and realize that even with how far he has come, especially given all of the artificial, intentional, and exhaustive barriers put before him, there is still a long way to go. Indeed, until those statistics from the Bureau of Labor and Statistics, as well as the studies and research from and other organizations and institutions vastly improve and show a much more evenly distributed trending among all groups, there is a long way to go.

As I continue to reflect on this, I become even more aware that regardless of whether one was brought here against their will centuries ago, immigrated here a half-century ago, or just came here yesterday, while we are not all from here, again we are all of here. We are all of here. In the spirit of that second son, that perception of somehow being less than still exists. And that is the greatest challenge to overcome.

So, to those who say, "I made it, why can't you?" Or, "We made it. Why can't you all?" Or worse, "The past is the past, get over it." I say go back and re-read your history, our history, this country's history. Do your best to realize the immense magnitude of what occurred. Take any point in your own life when you felt even marginally mistreated, victimized, rejected, or not seen, and magnify that by millions and centuries.

Here is a somewhat unorthodox way of looking at it. Watch a news program where they show a man being hit or robbed or viciously beaten. This man did nothing wrong. He was just in the wrong place at the wrong time, and he was attacked. He could even be an older man, or a smaller man. His attackers could be bigger or just more, or many. How would you feel watching him get beaten? Now picture a woman, or older lady, or young girl being attacked, beaten, even assaulted, perhaps by multiple attackers. She did nothing wrong, just in the wrong place at the wrong time. Take a moment and be in the moment. How would you feel? Now imagine that this attacked man, or this assaulted woman was your friend, or even your relative. How would you feel? Now picture all of this happening daily and being completely legal, even normal. How would you feel? Now magnify this by millions and centuries.

The main reasons that the actions occurred were due to the perception of certain people being "better" than others, or other people not worth as much as others. The laws changed, but the perceptions still linger to a significant extent. To be clear, many of those like, and from, the second son have "made it." Progress is undeniable. It is everywhere. But there is still a long way to go. Perception and reality.

To those who say, "I/We made it, what about you?" I say that while you may or may not have had help, you certainly were not weighted down with the burdens and heaviness of all the challenges that faced others who did not look like you. Unless you are Native American or Indigenous, your ancestors willingly and intentionally came to this country to begin a better life. Regardless of whatever prejudice they faced, you were never light years behind. In your own country you were never light years behind. Rich or poor, you were never light years behind. Regardless of if you were from here or of here, that perception did not exist for you. And you were never light years behind. Ever. Do I believe that things will eventually even out more broadly? Yes. Eventually, and with a lot of hard work. As I mentioned earlier, the signs are everywhere. The proof is everywhere. It's happening now, and has been, and will continue to. Whether you are an "initial" immigrant - a descendant of that second son - or fresh and new, you are of here. And although started much further back, are now catching up. We are catching up. We will catch up. Of that I have no doubt.

# CHAPTER 15

So where am I now? How am I with all this? I am good with this. I am good with me. I am very proud to be who and what I am. I am proud to be Nigerian. I am proud of that culture and heritage. I am proud to be of that line and people, specifically the Igbo people. We are rich with tradition and honor, history and culture. Of what I truly know of it, I know through my parents. Their story is my story. And theirs is the story. When my daughter was very young, and I told her that I, and so she is Nigerian, and that her grandparents were born and raised there, she smiled broadly. The word that she used to describe it was "exotic." That drove my own broad smile, then and now.

As I further reflect, I wonder if I was ever ashamed of my Nigerian heritage. As I gather my memories and experiences, I realize that the answer to that is, and always has been "No, not at all." I am aware that in my quest to fit in, my then desire to be less different, I just did not embrace it enough. Not nearly enough. Ironically, the pull to differentiate myself is greater now than I feel it has ever been. I look at my children and see how effortlessly they carve out their own unique presence, and style, and I marvel. Indeed, I've sought out their advice and counsel to "help" me on this journey of self-discovery with putting myself in a position to prioritize and permit myself my own ambitions. They offer guidance and patience, and again I marvel.

I am also proud to be an American. I cannot deny the greatness of this country that I was raised in, and have always been a part of. Is it perfect? No. Is it flawed? Yes. There have been tragedies and pain since its very inception. However, there has also been growth and progress, change and evolution. Hope. And in all of these elements lies the potential for limitless possibilities and boundless opportunities. Indeed, I have seen many so far, and am openly awaiting more to come. I think, feel, and believe that the generations to come, my children, will do wonders. Barriers will break, walls will fall, and second sons will catch up, and as a people, excel.

Once again, I am an immigrant son of immigrant parents. I am a Nigerian. I am an American. I am an African American Man of Color. I am a Black man. I am who I am, within and throughout. I am of here. I am home.

# EPILOGUE

### *My onyx ring.*

Oh yeah! My ring. So, as I wrote regarding my original onyx ring, after our shared readings, and when I was still very much reflecting on all that had occurred, both externally and internally, I did some extensive (very extensive) research in order to replace it. I found a place (or store) online that had what looked to be the exact shape and style of my original onyx. I went out and got my finger sized, just to make sure that it would fit perfectly. I was happy when I placed the order for the replacement, and looked forward to once again wearing it proudly. The fact is that I wear very little jewelry. In high school, for a time, when I was growing and changing, I wore a fake gold earring. It was "clipped" on to the bottom of my earlobe, as there was no way that my parents would let me get my ear pierced. Truth be told, I really wasn't pushing to get my ear pierced. I just wanted to wear the earring and look "cool" around school. The clip was so tight that the pain just didn't go away. In fact, I was actually glad when the day was over before practice when I could take it off. And there are other stories of not-so-real jewelry that I wore, and their effects, but I'll save that for another time.

When I asked for the gold onyx for my 18th birthday, I was not wearing any other jewelry at all, and the ring had meaning to it, which made it feel right. Later that year I received a gold necklace from my mother for Christmas. I believe that it was originally hers, as opposed to something that she had gone out and shopped for me. This made it more special. The necklace had a pendant on it in the form of a cross. The cross had a dove in the center of it. I had never seen anything like it before, and have not seen anything like it since. It's beautiful. These two pieces of jewelry were the only two things that I wore for years. This is my style. And who I am. The meaning was paramount. I did not take these off, ever, unless I absolutely had to. They have true, deep, personal meaning. I later added only my wedding band to this, again because of the monumental meaning.

When I received the new onyx that I had ordered to replace my original one, I was so excited. When I opened the box and saw it, I was equally disappointed. The size of the stone was wrong, and so was the overall shape, which was more of a rectangle, and flat. It was not what was pictured online. And they sent me an extra piece of jewelry, which was a beaded black bracelet. Why? Who knows. Perhaps they thought that I'd like the larger stone (nope) and would appreciate the additional bracelet (nope). I decided to wear the ring and see if it would (or could) grow on me. I tried. It didn't. After some time, I just took it off. And put it back into the case that it came in, right next to the bracelet. I've checked on it a couple of times, and it's actually turned colors (not good at all). I've done some more research, and it turns out that I found a local jeweler who can shape and size a new onyx ring and set it in the exact way that I want. The price is very expensive.

However, due to life and the many courses that it takes, I am now wearing a ring that my wife gave to me. It's a very long story. Very long. The new ring speaks to me of new beginnings. I wear it now, with my necklace and cross pendant, as well as my wedding band. I do not take them off. Again, I wear very little jewelry intentionally. The meaning of these items is very deeply rooted in who I am. As I continue to grow, change and evolve, my identity will no doubt continually advance as well. Which is a good thing. This journey, my journey, will continue.